Bachelor Pad

Bachelor Pad

Stephen Kampa

WAYWISER

First published in 2014 by

THE WAYWISER PRESS

Bench House, 82 London Road, Chipping Norton, Oxon OX7 5FN, UK
P.O. Box 6205, Baltimore, MD 21206, USA
http://waywiser-press.com

Editor-in-Chief
Philip Hoy

Senior American Editor
Joseph Harrison

Associate Editors
Dora Malech Eric McHenry Clive Watkins Greg Williamson

Copyright © Stephen Kampa, 2014

A CIP catalogue record for this book is available from the British Library

ISBN 978-1-904130-58-1

Printed and bound by
T.J. International Ltd., Padstow, Cornwall, PL28 8RW

Acknowledgments

I'd like to thank the following journals for first publishing poems:

Birmingham Poetry Review: "Bourbon Aubade," "The Forbidden Experiment"
Briar Cliff Review: "Wake"
Christianity and Literature: "Life of the Party"
First Things: "Wasted Time"
The Hopkins Review: "Trying to Pick Up Women at the Craft Fair"
Measure: "Double Features"
Poetry Northwest: "The Ghosts of Water," "Plenty to Him," "The Pocket Watch," "Watering the Garden (Till It Bursts Into Flame)"
Raritan: "The Gift," "Phlebotinum," "Walking Home Sober"
River Styx: "Small Change"
Smartish Pace: "The One Idea," "One Table Over"
St. Katherine Review: "First Gig"
Sewanee Theological Review: "The Album at the World's End"
Subtropics: "Near the Threshold"
Unsplendid.com: "Hand Signals," "Perforated for Ease of Separation"
Yale Review: "Bachelor Pad," "During the Hymn of Commitment"

"Small Change" won the 2011 *River Styx* International Poetry Contest. I offer thanks to that journal, and particularly to Richard Newman, for the continued support and thanks to B. H. Fairchild for selecting my poem.

The poems published in *Poetry Northwest* were awarded the 2011 Theodore Roethke Prize. I offer thanks to that journal, and particularly to Kevin Craft, for the support and encouragement.

I also owe a debt of gratitude to ART342 for the time and space they gave me to work on this book. Special thanks to Jim and Wendy Franzen for their generosity and support, and extra special thanks to Amy Reckley for her knowledgeability, good humor, and hospitality while I was in Fort Collins and for her ever increasing awesomeness in the years since.

Mary Jo Salter has been nothing short of saintly in her patience and encouragement. Everything I write has benefited from her intelligence, wisdom, and marvelous sense of music – even the poems I chose, in rare bursts of mercy, not to foist upon her with pleas for help. Mary Jo: thank you, thank you, thank you.

I'm deeply indebted to the whole Waywiser crew. Phil Hoy, with his brilliant interviews for Between the Lines and his publication of writers through Waywiser, continues to be a servant of and hero for poetry. I also count myself luckier than lucky to have had a poet I admire, Joseph Harrison, work with me to make this a better book.

I would like to thank the people who put up with me, and sometimes put me up, during the later stages of writing this book – my mother, my father and stepmother, the incomparable and irreplaceable Scott Durden, Mike and DeNae Hiltner – as well as those without whose good company and counsel I wouldn't make it: my three brothers, Mary DiSalvo, Gretchen Fierke, Jessica Flood, Fred Fronauer, Will Healy, Teresina Lyman, John McComb, Matthew Richardson, and Connie Walker. The musicians of both my youth and my adulthood in Daytona Beach have given me much good advice about art and the life of the artist, and I thank them for it now and always. The usual suspects at the Sewanee Writers' Conference each deserve my gratitude and have it. Finally, there are many people who peek out from the pages of this book in one way or another – sometimes for being a part of a poem, and sometimes for being a part of my life – and if I haven't named them, it isn't because I don't know who they are; I trust they know who they are, too, and how important they are to me. I believe love is a house with many mansions – many *kinds* of mansion, in fact – and in the house of mine, they each have their own.

Contents

At Home

Hitherto all things that have bin nam'd, were approv'd of God to be very good: lonelines is the first thing which Gods eye nam'd not good . . . And here alone *is meant alone without woman; otherwise* Adam *had the company of God himself, and Angels to convers with; all creatures to delight him seriously, or to make him sport. God could have created him out of the same mould a thousand friends and brother* Adams *to have bin his consorts; yet for all this till* Eve *was giv'n him, God reckon'd him to be alone.*

– Milton, "Tetrachordon"

Homer at Home

He couldn't, after all, be said to dwell in
A kingly castle when she gave him hell in
Every regard. Her tirades left him shaking:

She'd launch into the thousand hardships making
Their match a disappointment – him a slob,
And all the drinking, and his job, what *job*? –

Until she ran him down and drove him mad.
The years of hectoring, the ill he had
To suffer – all of it now made him feel

That getting hitched was his Achilles' heel.
Not that she hadn't been worn down by his
Unbroken strings of broken promises,

The winding yarns he spun in his defense;
Not that she didn't harbor a looming sense
That somewhere, somehow, both their ships had sunk

(The weaving home at three A.M. dead drunk)
And bitters were the sea they now must swim in
(His frank entanglements with foreign women) –

So she admired the clean audacity
Of her old schoolgirl friend Penelope
Who, with a new man, knew no end to hope:

Penny had found it in her to elope
And now sent postcards ("What've you got to lose?")
From ports ("To die for!") on her wedding cruise.

Homer, meanwhile, grew derelict with age.
One word. *One word.* To ward off the blank page,
He started with the most instinctive: *Rage.*

Around Town

Plenty to Him

Already there were signs
That they would not have sex or something more –
    They dropped unwitty lines
Like decks of cards scattered across the floor,
    Then needed to repeat them
Because they couldn't hear above the bar's
Boisture; they ordered wings, but didn't eat them;
    They didn't like the same
Books, board games, wines, or punch lines; after hours
Of chitchat, he could not dredge up her name.

    They tried a second date.
She bitched about her boyfriend (how'd he miss
    That bombshell?) and the fate
Of indie rock; half-drunk, she dragged a kiss
    Across his whiskery cheek
And said good night, which left him feeling – blue?
Bald and unhappy, he consigned the week
    To hopeless mopery
And hair growth infomercials: nothing new.
His mother offered, "Plenty of fish in the sea."

    He hated that expression –
Useful advice for piscatory flops,
    Perhaps, but not to freshen
The salty depths of grief to which love drops
    Back in the lace-hemmed wake
Of disappointment – but it brought to mind
That miracle where Jesus had to break
    Five borrowed loaves of bread,
Divide two puny fish, and somehow find
A way to feed five thousand, which he did.

He wanted more detail
So he could picture Jesus round up, bone
        By bone and scale by scale,
More fish from nothing; that had never been
        His take on plenitude,
It smacked of sideshow magic, and he wondered
If that first crowd's sophisticates found it crude.
        His paradigm of plenty
Had as its source the afternoon he'd blundered
Upon a pair of streams hid in the twenty

        Acres of wooded land
Behind his uncle's house. He couldn't tell
        From where he'd had to stand
Whether they ran exactly parallel,
        But he'd imagined lying
Between them, belly down – he'd barely fit,
They streamed so close together – and, while trying
        To still his full heart's beating,
Felt intimations of the infinite
There in the nearness of their never meeting.

Hand Signals

I'm sitting in the city park and watching
    Bright windows' patchwork quilt the dark,
Thinking how soon it will be cold, and feeling
    Sorry I have no hand to hold;
A streetwise palmist's patter fills the air,

    A traffic cop's curt whistle shrills –
They don't disturb the hipster thumping bongos
    Here in the grass. The cop's hands jump
And circle, guiding cars in loose formations
    Past neon signs for a masseuse.

This is my secret charge: I wait for someone
    To come and change me, but it's late,
And no one comes. I think, *Who needs the hassle?*
    I'd rather be a man who reads
The signs and makes connections by himself.

    Across the street, the intersection's
Walk signal's amber hand is slowly flashing
    As if to say, *No, wait, don't go,*
Or maybe *High five! Way to lie!,* or nothing,
    Content instead to wave goodbye.

First Gig

Love become muscle, muscle all the world
He lives for now, our hero – ginned and girled
Into a pop-rock stupor high as stars –
Lies in his bed and listens to the cars
Honk with the pure frustration of the many
Who haven't gotten any
Tonight while he, the lucky schmuck, enjoys
The sweaty equipoise
Of Tina, Yoga Queen,
Who rocks on top of him because she's seen
Him slap lead bass tonight amidst the bustle
Of barroom spotlights, smoke, and noise;
So now both world and love contract to muscle.

He sat so wide-eyed when she dropped her bra
That no one could predict how little awe
He'll come to feel in later years when faced
With just such women, having lost the taste
For kissing naked strangers; but he'll kiss them,
Then screw them, then dismiss them,
Since that's what rock stars' groupies dig. He'll play
His part, a bit blasé,
And one day when he's lost
His love for music, he'll recall some tossed-
Off wisdom from his mentor: "Off a third?
No problem. Might sound good. But say
You're off a half-step . . . worst note ever heard."

So not all misses were as good as miles –
Near ones were worse. He learned from jazzophiles
To whom his mentor brought him, and he wrote
Down all their riffs: "I'll play an awkward note
Eight or nine times, and it stops sounding wrong;
By then, it's part of the song. . . . "
"There *aren't* wrong notes! Harmony has no chaff.

You're never more than half
A step from sounding great. . . . "
"Mid-solo, and you're empty – what now? *Wait*.
Silence is music, too." With each addition
He scribbled in his sheaf of staff
Paper, he reaped more fruit as a musician.

The sole experiences he'll think profounder
Came from the nights he went out gigging flounder
With his stepfather, who instructed him
On how to shine his lantern through the dim
Water to search for amber starburst eyes.
"Because a flounder lies
Flat, buried in the sand, you need to find
His eyes and strike *behind*
Them, hard; but if you pick
The wrong side of the eyes to stab, you'll stick
Your gig in the empty sand ahead of him
And lose your chance. Keep that in mind. . . . "
Before his eyes, these memories will swim

On gig-nights when the stage lights scintillate
Reflections in the eyes of fans who wait
Nearest him in the bar where he's been booked:
The gorgeous girls all watch him gigging, hooked.
He'll daydream of one catch so big the ship
Floundered throughout its trip,
Then of another fabled boatload where
The fishnets didn't tear
Beneath a record haul;
And last, he'll recollect that jazzer's small
Smile upon being challenged to defend
The No-Wrong-Note Approach. "That's fair . . .
Music's all *motion*. It matters where you *end*."

Some resolution. While our bassist smokes
Cheap ganja, Tina cracks a few weak jokes
About his tokens of affection, closing
The door behind her. Split screen: Hero, dozing,
Yet half-entranced by how his life has changed,
A standard rearranged
For edgy chords, fresh words, and accolades;
Girl, hoping she evades
Her cabbie's rearview gaze
The whole way home, now certain time betrays
Even the freest spirits to being haunted
Indefinitely by the gray shades
Of almost having what they'd almost wanted.

Life of the Party

The Son of Man came eating and drinking, and you
say, "Here is a glutton and a drunkard, a friend of
tax collectors and 'sinners.'"
                                        – Luke 7:34

First he arrived with top-notch beer, remarking
        He'd found some decent parking
A few blocks down; next thing I know, he's playing
        A banjo with dismaying
Skill for a guy who claims his "music bone"
        Is broken, that he's tone
Deaf and could never read a proper score;
        And now he's on the floor,
Cross-legged, near a crass blonde, wetly blinking,
        Who's doggedly been drinking
Herself into a venomous redress
        Of red forgetfulness –
Really, what moron thought she could afford
        That umpteenth one she poured? –
And now he's holding, to the girl's relief,
        The wine glass of her grief,
And offering, sotto voce, while they sit,
        To drink the last of it.

Trying to Pick Up Women at the Craft Fair

What's more humiliating
Than knowing you would fake
A love of hand-carved dolls
To score a chance at dating
Some hottie? One mistake
In terminology
(They're "figurines") and she
Will stop returning calls.

Probably you can think
Of worse scenarios
Only because you've tried
The "Pardon me *(blink blink)*,
You've *such* a chiseled nose,
Are you a model?" ruse
Too often when you cruise
Car shows. Access denied.

Then there's the Roadside-Crouch-
And-Clutch-Your-Guts routine.
Maybe some cute chick stops,
You end up on her couch,
But there it ends: the scene
Breaks when you ask to crash
At her place. Your panache
Gets you one stiff hug, tops.

Still, here you play the part
Of tchotchke connoisseur;
You chat girls up, they let you
Down. Somewhere near the heart
Of Aisle Sixteen (a blur
Of boxwood jesters, grooms,
And tipplers), one broad booms
She doesn't really *get* you.

Your last chance drives away.
Your failures are a ton
Of woodchips. And the deft
Strokes of the knife? Each day
That pares you down to one
Less possibility
For happiness. You see?
Life whittles. You're what's left.

Where You See Her

.bove all, clothe yourselves with love, which binds
everything together in perfect harmony.
                    – Colossians 3:14

But in the end, he knew, this would be foreplay
To the main event when she'd take him to the cleaners.
                    – Anthony Hecht

Maybe the Laundromat. Between the final
Spin cycle and the wet slog to the dryer,
            While leafing through the dreary
            Ads in a bad gazette,

Your shoulders sticking to a chair's cracked vinyl,
You glance up and she's walking past. You squint.
            You knit your brows. You can't
            Remember why you got

That blouse – some long-gone anniversary? –
But it seems changed; it crackles with a cooler,
            More cultivated color.
            She's ditched the six-inch heel.

Although you swear that you were never sorry
For dumping all her presents at the Good Will,
            You're not sure any good will
            Come of it, and you feel

Stupid for slouching here in a tattered A-shirt
After she bought you all those pricey silk
            Polos; you whirl to sulk
            In your gym shorts and flip-flops

While she floats by, possessed and self-assured,
And you remember that you felt this dorky
            When you flung back her door key
            The night she called the cops.

Glad to be cut loose, right? She cramped your style.
Yet seeing her now is like waking thirsty late
      At night and getting out
      Of bed to find some water –

You gasp at the cold shock of kitchen tile
On your bare sole because you still forget
      Your left sock has a hole
      The size of a lost quarter.

One Table Over

How distant Christ's divine *Tetelestai*
    Is from this couple's public spat.
No cussing, cuffs, or tears – it's through the sly
      Pause of his inattention,
Her nail-thin mouth, their terse snit's tit for tat,
That they are intimating their dissension.

Maybe they've stumbled on some cornerstone
    Assumption they no longer share;
Maybe a sudden cross exchange has grown
      Into this practiced chill;
Or maybe something dumb has split the pair –
Who spilled the beer or who will pay the bill.

It's such a gamble, loving one another.
    If any couple could foresee
The numberless petty means by which they'd smother
      All natural affection
As years go by – the routine perfidy,
The vicious bickering over which direction

They're headed on the highway as they barrel
    Past the right exit, the forgotten
Birthdays and reasons, the retreats to sterile
      Chitchat, the kaffeeklatsch
Marriage becomes – they'd never throw their lot in
With lifelong vows. Only a god could watch

The piercingly precise guilt tapestry
    Of forthright wrongs and fifth-rate pleas
For more forgiveness, each indecency
      In manifold detail –
This quarreling couple's knife-edged pleasantries,
My glib projection of the ways they fail –

And still fall hopelessly in love. Here's Christ
    Inviting Judas to a meal.
This is before he hung there, bargain-priced,
    Nailed to the blood-soaked wood,
While Judas hanged himself; before the deal
For thirty pieces of silver, understood

As what a man would cost; before the rage
    Sparked by that alabaster jar,
Nard worth three hundred times the daily wage;
    Before the piecemeal theft
From the communal coffer. Here, now, are
Judas and Jesus, and there's nothing left

Unseen by this one who will be betrayed –
    He feels the last kiss in the first –
And still he offers bread his mother made,
    Gives one more cup of wine
To quench what will become a quenchless thirst.
He cleans his feet. . . . So this is the divine.

"You got this one? Last time, I grabbed the check,"
    The man says. Smug. A little snide.
He leans in, but she flinches, guards her neck
    From his prospective kiss.
"Aw, Jesus, Beth!" he barks. "Let's talk outside!"
"Fine," she says. "*Fine.*" Which means, *You'll pay for this.*

Small Change

Nothing expressly intimate nor strange
Occurred to us: no sparks, no psychic links,
No star-crossed destinies. You brought me drinks,
We bartered jokes, you handed me my change,

And now you bartend farther up the street.
Why this inestimable wistfulness?
Why hope when sozzled patrons deliquesce
From their eccentric barstools or the sleet

Rattles its nails against the windowpanes,
After the party's made its bourbon-flushed
Dispersal and the bar grows dark and hushed –
Tips counted, chairs all tabled – there remains

In you an unpronounced uncertainty,
The feeling that you missed a crucial word
In some conclusive sentence overheard?
Why think that, driving home, you think of me?

Even if our exchanges were the least
Of common currencies – a courtesy
Embellished with brief mischief, jeux d'esprit
Informed by decorous desires – we pieced

Together from them something worthy of
This keen encomium, each word a token
Of an affection spoken and unspoken:
If not quite love, then like enough to love.

That's my two cents, of course, but think how much
Those two cents mean, how much one can derive
From just one coin: a jukeboxed forty-five
Or canned pop, sure, but when a girl would clutch

A dime between her knees because her mom
Had warned her, "If this hits the ground, you use it
To call me," so she wouldn't, you know, *lose it*,
A coin could save her honor during prom;

The drifting boaters who revived the old
Coin-in-the-fuse-box trick and fled the sound
Before the year's worst storm ran them aground
Each, to the man, ecstatically extolled

The coin conducting them to shoreside calm;
And there are still anarchic foreign states
Where flipping coins decide the inmates' fates –
Their futures shimmer in a despot's palm.

More shimmers. Stand a penny upright on
Its edge and flick it: watch the sudden planet,
So small a single fingernail would span it,
Whir with the movement of its copper dawn

As images from both sides flicker, blend,
And separate until the game adjourns,
The world stops spinning, and the whole thing turns
Thin, flat, and cold again, its moving end

Given some grand finale soundtrack flair
When, as the coin falls down, it rattles faster –
Rolls on a kettledrum that mean disaster
Has struck as now that coin becomes the fare

Squished in a dead man's mouth while his kids squabble
Over the will. How better make the global
Local or render humble pennies noble
Than transmute every coin to Charon's obol?

If any given lepton can outleap
Its market sense, although we'll never join
Together like two sides of the same coin,
We still have something valuable to keep:

Our personal account of common pleasures,
Lockbox mementos we let no one else see.
The *sou* in *souvenir* must mean, dear Kelsey,
That memory rewards with hidden treasures,

So I'm remembering our numberless
Exchanges as if I were someone gifted
Enough to recollect each coin that's sifted,
At some point, through his hands; and I confess

That part of me, at least, has learned to settle
For kindly offered sympathies of speech
And sportive gestures, pondering in each
The pinch, the mite, the twinge of precious metal.

The Necklace

Here at the end,
Even an ingénue could reconstruct
        The things that happened from
The maelstrommed sheets, the pillows jettisoned,
    The wakeful state to which she'd come:
            Last night they'd fucked.

Follow the trail
Clewed out – loose button threads, a bra strap snapped –
        Back to the kitchen sink
Where cork and corkscrew writhe beside the stale
    Red wine that she'll no longer drink;
            Spills have recapped

Their steep descent
In topographic splotches of maroon.
        Red cairns of candle wax,
Dry tablelands, shy girl on couch. She's spent
    The morning following their tracks
            To this, and soon

She'll have to rise
And clean the counters, brush away the night's
        Crumbs, kiss that ingénue
Goodbye. Her ship has sailed. Her captain tries
    The shower's acoustics, scaling anew
            His withering heights.

Who sees her pure
Distraction? Last night she'd been so insistent.
        She cries. Her fingers drift
To the hickeys on her throat as if they were
    A necklace she'd received, a gift
            From someone distant.

Wasted Time

You'd think that after New Year's boozy kisses,
Back-slapping, and effusions in confetti,
The last hors-d'oeuvres and passes at the Mrs.
Beneath the hanging cardboard amoretti,

Time would relax, agree to stay a while,
Hang up his sandals, lay aside his shift,
And sleep it off until the chamomile
Light has suffused the blinds; but Time's too swift

For *that* one, you palooka, look at how
Steady he is, rock-solid, never mind
The rocking on his feet, he's sober *now*,
He's at the door, he says, *You've been too kind*,

I'll take the wheel, stop whining, fairest creatures,
Been doing this since Remus founded Rome,
And concentrates on hardening his features,
Jangling his keys, ready to drive us home.

Walking Home Sober

After three months of drinking hard,
Tonight I skipped the eggnog, mulled wine, ale,
    And felt much better having barred
Myself from alcohol: wise, hearty, hale,
I didn't pinch the hostess, didn't puke
Or pass out on the sofa, and I left
    Before receiving a rebuke
For begging off, not up to getting effed.

Outside, it's peaceful cold and stars,
Austere somehow despite inflatable
    Snowmen in yards, the empty cars
And Christmas lights and, maybe worst of all,
Those wiry reindeer silhouettes that blink
Their heads in twelve-watt pantomimes of eating;
    And I, not stultified by drink,
Seize on how grating is each season's greeting.

What is all this but one more stab
At fullness, one more tinsel-thin attempt
    To salvage gladness from the drab
And selfish disaffection, savage contempt,
And rage that are this age's gifts to us?
Sober like this, I almost understand
    The parable of emptiness
I read in *The Collection of Stone and Sand*.

An old Zen master served his guest –
A quizzical professor – some green tea,
    But poured too much as if to test
The teacher's patience; and when finally
The man cried, "Stop! The cup is overfull!"
He said, "And so are you: your mind's made up,
    Spilling with speculations. Fool!
To master Zen, you need to empty your cup."

My pastor says we clench our fists
Tightly because we think God means to snatch
    The dram-sized world we dream exists
When, in truth, only open hands can catch
The world God wants to fill them with, the one
That David glimpsed first in the meadow grass,
    Waters of rest, and paths he'd run
When just a shepherd kid; he'd had to pass

    Through valleys reeking of what died
Unresurrectably in them before
    God welcomed David back inside,
Uncovered steaming plates, and rose to pour
Anointing oil on him. Cup overflowing,
The king could feel God's giddy love distilling
    Into the final taste of knowing
That being full depends on who is filling.

    Okay, whatever. Moral tales
Are more tall tales than they're immortal signs.
    I wish I could define what ails
Me such that beers and eggnogs, shots and wines
Have been my ways of working through the weak
Sense of dissatisfaction now fermented
    Into these fine despairs that pique
Dismal contentions in the discontented.

    There's plenty here to make me cranky:
Successive unsuccessful dates that hone
    My hankering for hanky-panky;
The vapid job, the dining out alone;
The nearly vacant church pews; and the fact
My father's father died this summer, leaving
    Behind a widow and a cracked
Shot glass that leaks as if the glass were grieving.

It comes to this: all flesh is flesh.
We know that. How surprising, then, there'd be
    In each yard on this block a crèche,
That hymn to incarnation. Now I see
They're bodiless. Some fools – the neighborhood's
Own homegrown pranksters, or some drunken strangers? –
    Have jumped the fences, grabbed the goods,
And left behind a wake of empty mangers.

Sleepless with Reruns

The Forbidden Experiment

Words alone are certain good.
      – Yeats

Step One: You steal two infants, isolate
      Them on an uninhabited
Island, have robots feed them. Step Two: Wait.
            Will they progress from grunts to gibberish
                  Until there forms
            What all the linguists wish,
                  A new tongue with its own syntactic norms?

What would their first word be? A crunchy noun,
      A scraggly verb? Would they develop
A broad phonemic palette, or one stripped down
            To only the essential human hums,
                  Plus the odd croak?
            I'd hope their language comes
                  With systems of inflections so baroque

That even the hard-bitten behaviorists
      Feel smitten with the implication
That something beautifully innate exists
            Within a person and permits him speech –
                  The holy lives
            And breathes within our reach
                  In dental clicks and glottal fricatives! –

But I am not convinced, and that is not
      The question anyway. We want
To know if we are good. If we were brought
            As children into a secluded glade,
                  Would we still grow
            Into the bored, dismayed
                  Adults who don't know what they just won't know,

39

Or would we all become the luminaries
    That we suspect ourselves to be
In some inviolate place? Maybe it varies.
        You lose the trashy daytime talk shows, ads,
            Sports, politics,
        Pulp fiction, diet fads,
            Frauds, alcoholics, fondlers, crack-heads, tricks,

And sure, you might end up a decent type.
    As for the origin of language,
Psammetichus of Egypt took a swipe
        At that one: when he wanted to unearth
            The world's first race,
        He took two boys at birth
            And had them raised in a deserted place;

A shepherd brought them milk, but never broke
    The silence he was forced to keep.
The ruler thought that when the children spoke,
        They'd use our most instinctive tongue, displaying
            By what they said
        Which ancients did the saying.
            Their first word was the Phrygian word for bread,

Which solved the matter. Here's what I would know:
    How long before those children hit
On other words, the hard ones? Did they show
        Alarming skill in filling the world with dread
            Curses once driven
        To use them? Was that bread
            Demanded, offered, taken, shared, or *given*?

What fine distinctions for those famous wards
   Whose native language was the silence
We started with! But they learned many words:
      Our nameless boys grew fluent in the breaking
        Of one another's
      Hearts. Simple. Just like taking
        Candy from babies, children from their mothers.

Insomnia Cinema

At midnight, nothing stops
Him from imagining his bedroom furniture,
Nightstand detritus, books, life, everything,
Are stagehand-damaged props
In some low-budget feature –
Tearjerker, screwball comedy, or middling
Farce, God only knows.

Of course, he could be acting
In a triumphant star
Vehicle, one complete
With heady long shots, a string-heavy score,
And a leading lady like Hedy Lamarr –
Rivetingly distracting,
She'd salvage the camp plot
With complicated schemes or dry-wit salvos
None the poorer
For her commanding figure –
But probably it's horror.

He vies with sleep and views
The marvelously detailed storyboards
Of Insomnia Cinema, Inc. –
The montage of his own romantic failures,
History's mangled hoards,
The noose of nightly news
Tightening in a blink –
Till minutes seem to hold full years,
The way an infant's ear
Can hear, in instants, epochs talk. He stalls,
Recalling underlined
Passages from the oversweet
Novel that he's been reading, unamused
By its cheap fairy tale re-adaptation
(It oozes what he calls

Silent regrimmination –
He bought his copy used).
Its sleeve-worn faith that goodness never fails,
That "warmth" should "radiate"
From every sheet,
Strikes him as false, since even fairy tales
Conceal the laity's fear
That, crumb by crumb, we find
Pain is the bread we eat.

He glances at his gray T.V.
Soon he must choose which movies
He means to watch: those looping
Endlessly through his head –
A cinematic Möbius
Strip he alone can see
Unspooling – or the slop that the unsleeping
Millions click on in bed,
Those late-night flicks abundant
With iterations of the same old phantom
Or zippered teratoids
And tin-can androids
Whipping through space on asteroids
And premises as flimsy
As onionskin. They're all replayed,
He thinks, ad infinitum;
Yet when he feels he's finally abandoned
All hope, he still hopes whimsy
Hides wisdom, that the oddest
Logical wrinkle
(The sort of howler that would rankle
Him anywhere but in a modest
B-movie) might provide
A wormhole through the void
Or trapdoor into hidden chambers

Where a symbolic torch's flame bares
The mysteries to light.
Maybe he's just afraid
Of this suspicious fact: the tighter
The narrative, the more defined its shape,
The less that anyone is likely to escape,
And since he fears not being even
Remotely in control
Of his own character, one lasting
Enough to let in heaven,
He has to ask: if perfect love casts out
Fear, who will play which role,
And who will do the casting?

The two spooked eyes – wide, white,
Like the last two hosts on a blackened paten –
That make him flinch,
Startled, aren't eyes, but stare unblinking
From what he might put on
To try to pass the night:
A video cassette,
Which ought to mean, in French,
A little broken thing.

Large Cast

My vegetable love should grow
Vaster than empires, and more slow.
        – Marvell

After they discover the alien embedded
      in a block of Arctic ice, they end
up spending the first third of the movie (*The Thing from*
      Another World, 1951)
spluttering back and forth in the classic scientist-
      equals-mind-and-army-guy-equals-
body dialogue about whether to unfreeze it.
      They're playing to all my weaknesses –
Theremin-soaked soundtrack, botanists in turtlenecks,
      a male lead whose face looks like a lump
you'd find behind a butcher's counter (and still he gets
      the girl!) – but what really beguiles me

is the large cast, the dozen or so people, most of
      whom make it, that trade their genial
joshes with an air of such sweet bonhomie that once
      again I wish, in classic viewer-
equals-nostalgic-outsider fashion, that I could
      enter an ensemble cast and be
partner to the patter, the pratfalls, and the endless
      innuendo of that era when
even a sci-fi thriller boasted a wit-filled script.
      O, Large Cast – who would want, after all,
a smaller one, a cast with even one less than this,
      a cast of two? Give me the comfort

of a dozen banterers, save me with twelve beaker-
      savvy scions of science because
someone goofs and thaws that sanguinary spaceman out;
      they kill him, although at first he seems
(because a vegetable) invincible. As for me,
      I'm thinking about all those stories

of cavemen frozen for millennia, how the past
      can be as distant as the arms of
any galaxy. Yesterday's mail brought a letter
      from my ex, and today I am still
considering if and how to respond. Sure, we hit
      it off, but off and on; on an off

day, either of us might become an emotional
      troglodyte or psychopath or plain
old monster. We parted on the classic blinding-flash-
      of-light-equals-cathartic-rocket-
crash-equals-insight bit. We lingered on the credits.
      But isn't every ending the same?
Sparks wisp to ash, and stars disperse as dust. Anyway,
      let me mention how our brainiacs
finally aced their beast: they incinerated him
      with electricity, but only
after their first attempt with kerosene and flare gun
      misfired. Different method, same old flames.

The Ghosts of Water

Offer tears to mourn the water-ghosts,
and water-ghosts take them, glimmering.
– Meng Chiao

We're water that remembers . . .
– John Hollander

Maybe a mist along the windowsill
Appears from nowhere, a sporadic leak
Puddles beneath the sink, wet footprints still

Darken the bathmat after you've been gone
All day at work; maybe the water stains
Bleeding across the ceiling spell oblique

Warnings to those who read them, and the drains
Gurgle their urgent Hottentot before
Receding to a silence all the more

Ominous for the night-dew on the lawn;
But these are fears of which we rarely speak.
I've heard they slither underneath the door

Or dribble through the pipes and reappear
Glistening in the kitchen; as they pore
Over your mouth, breathe wetly in your ear,

They run damp fingers through your shampooed hair.
Your beaded forehead proves that they were there.
And this is not to mention where the rain

Comes in. Yet you, perhaps, have never faced
Such longing, such condensed expressions of
Something you might mistake for muted love

Transmuted into water drops like tears –
Their rancor has distilled into this skill
For squeezing from you terribly misplaced

Compassion. When did their burbled coos begin
To drown out sound? They want what all ghosts want.
Sixty percent of you has given in.

Double Features

The classic movie channel sometimes plays a pair
Of films the same leads starred in (Rogers and Astaire,
Flynn and de Havilland), so musicals might morph
To hardboiled noir – fedora'd gunmen guard a wharf
And punctuate the mist with pulsing cigarettes –
Or bland romantic comedies might cede their place
To pirates pirouetting through their rigged-up sets,
And everywhere those same two stars stand face to face,

Enchanted or entrapped (depending on the ending)
By passion so commanding, *our* love seems worth mending,
Something commendable – we share their magnanimity,
Their scripted grace, if not in praxis, then by proximity –
And we ignore the more appropriate connection:
Like them, we went from costars warbling warm aubades
After the nights spent trumpeting our predilection
For pas de deux, or lovers passed over by the gods

Of pained adieux, to moll and conman giving phony
Names to the feds and free rein to their acrimony,
Or pirates with their cutlasses drawn . . . what troubled creatures
We are, who now suspect each other's double features
And let our programs (onetime classics rereleased
For TV) do our talking for us, framed in black
And white. Most nights we take our cues from them, not least
In how we sleep: for twice as long and back to back.

Lana Turner's Bosom: An Assay

During the golden years in Hollywood,
The studio execs sought out the most
Distinctive figures, lilts, and miens from coast
　　To coast and cast them as the good
Housewife, the girl next door, the renegade
Seductress, trying to induce what best
Befit those droopy lids or that heaving breast
　　　　As the next great stars played
　　The parts for which they had been made.

Typecasting worked – why, even now you might
Remember Ava Gardner as the vamp
Par excellence, an unabashed sex champ –
　　And it could turn girls overnight
Into the nation's top box-office earners
Who could expect, in turn, a queenly cut
Of all the swag; but let's get back to what
　　　　Really lights my burners,
　　The bosoms – namely, Lana Turner's.

In Lana's film debut (a courtroom thriller
Titled, ironically, *They Won't Forget*),
She plays a Southern college-aged coquette
　　Accosted by an unknown killer
Who drops her down an elevator shaft
Within the first ten minutes of the feature;
Suspicion subsequently fells her teacher,
　　　　An urban Yankee graft
　　Sans country roots, but it's the craft

In post-production that I most admire.
The money shot's the one where Lana walks
In fleshly confidence through a packed block's
　　Milling parade crowd; her entire
Body exudes a healthy, sexual bounce.

Mervyn LeRoy affirmed once (and I'm with him)
That Lana Turner's bosom had "a rhythm
    All its own" – that flounce
  That pricks the movie's fiend to pounce –

And when he added music to the scene,
He prompted the composer of the score
To stress the rhythm of that thirty-four
    C bust in motion, and a teen
Sensation sizzled into fame in time!
I loved that chestnut and, in innocence,
Reviewed the relevant footage. My two cents?
    Delight can turn on a dime:
  The movie's based on a true crime,

I learned while watching, and the real-life victim,
A girl named Mary Phagan, was a mere
Thirteen years old when murdered. I can hear
    The whispers of a weary dictum –
Ars longa, vita brevis – while I browse
The literature: the man who went to trial,
One Leo Frank, stood firm in his denial
    Of knowledge of the hows
  Or whys, which only seemed to rouse

All of Atlanta's ire. Despite the case's
Weaknesses – circumstantial evidence,
Conflicting testimonies – his defense
    Suffered a series of disgraces
As a parade of witnesses cast aspersions
On Frank's good character: no one could save it
From affidavit after affidavit
    Describing his excursions
  Into a realm of frank perversions,

51

Sexual deviancies best left suggested
Rather than flatly stated; and as predicted,
Frank later was summarily convicted,
    Although the verdict was contested
Both in and out of court as through the news
The brawl about the tawdry facts became
More than a cry to clear a young man's name:
        It boiled down to views
    On Northern suasion, wealth, and Jews.

Reading it all now, I can hardly say
What really happened. Witnesses retracted
Their statements willy-nilly, mobs reacted –
    Iudicium dificile.
The commutation of Frank's sentence clinched
His fate: knight-vigilantes sprang him loose –
They kidnapped him from prison. With the noose
    Of Georgia justice cinched
    Around his neck, Frank was lynched.

I can't do justice to this complex story
(It took Steve Oney seven-hundred pages
And seventeen years' research in courageous
    Pursuit of his stone-quiet quarry,
The truth that he gives voice to in his book),
Although I do believe Frank's innocence;
But given such malevolent events,
    I think it's time I took
    A second, less presumptuous look

At who's most likely to be lost in this
Redaction: Mary Phagan. She devolved
To headlines as the linchpin in an unsolved
    Crime, then became the impetus
For one impetuous newsman to compose

A novelized account of what transpires
When Yankee profs can't master their desires,
    And then poor Mary rose
  To stardom in the tailored clothes

And sultry walk of sixteen-year-old Miss
Turner, until at last she comes to rest
Here in this poem, where I might divest
    Her of her last few essences
Of selfhood; and what spring to mind are old
Paintings where figures are reiterated
Across the canvas in an antiquated
    Stop motion: we behold
  The chains of subjects who have strolled

Up from the distant background to the fore,
The present, in a change that's nearly mystic –
They grow most lifelike when they're most artistic.
    Their closest selves impress us more
Than any shrouded by perspective's blur
Or scumbled fog. Just so, beneath the glaze
Of my long-drawn, appropriative gaze,
    You are whom I infer
  Now, Mary, never who you were.

I'll tell you where this poem was to start,
O, Reader: I'd imagined Hollywood,
Despite its turpitude, once understood
    That though you might adjust a part
In someone's hair or straighten teeth or shade
The hollows of a gorgeous woman's cheeks,
You limited yourself to minor tweaks;
    The groundwork had been laid.
  Some things are given; some things, made.

Our future stars, however, would be those
So plain and program-pliant that in truth
They only existed in the editing booth:
    Computer-generated nose,
Drag-and-drop jaw line, real-time boobs. No chance
For girls like Lana Turner, young and brimming
With unforced lustrousness. Their stars were dimming.
    Who'd film a countenance
    That hard to digitally enhance?

That contrast fails because it frames distortion
As more the province of the arts than life.
But life's distorted, friends, distortion's rife
    In being, it's our natural portion:
Remember all the witnesses who swore
First for and then against poor Leo Frank.
Remember Mary Phagan, mutely blank,
    Translated into lore
    And, finally, an evened score.

Here's my newfangled ending: once we're dead,
Men will inflect our names and pitch our voices.
A second wave will second-guess our choices.
    We'll all be reinterpreted –
Victims of circumstance, dupes of some fad.
Archived on YouTubes, Facebooks, and MySpaces,
We'll be our viewers' comments, and our faces,
    Whether for good or bad,
    Won't be the faces that we had.

Selective Memory

The DVD's main menu promises
Pizzazzy features if a viewer presses
The proper button, but I'm better off
Without them. Call me a barbarian,
But I still miss the hiss-prone VHS's
That I grew up with. (Nostalgia always wins –
At least, it used to.) Meanwhile, the disc spins:
A soundtrack twiddles its fifteen-second loop
While I lean back and polish off my bourbon.
I felt dry, dull, and horribly suburban
While watching my protagonists elope
Into wide fields of atmospheric light
And small, vague villages with cobblestones
And no hardscrabble times, no blights or stains,
A place so level you forget it's flat.
Here's a true story: once I wanted love
As cinematic as an ocean liner
Sinking with both the belle and winsome loner
Aboard, adored and sure to find a skiff,
Yet love familiar as a rolled-up sleeve;
Not everyone wants life that picturesque.
My ex enjoyed a film where two guys duke
It out barehanded on a burning deck:
"Oh yeah?" says one, unbuttoning his cuff.
"Yeah," sneers the other, tossing back some booze.
I rooted for the one we knew would lose –
I can admit this, I'm not a guy to mince
Words – partly out of pity, and in part
Because I'd realized I was a fill-in
Lover and longed to change into that villain
Who, if he couldn't keep the girl, would risk
Death trying to. Instead, when X proposed
That facts were facts and needed to be faced,
I thought about how she, a fan of brutal
Final showdowns, would gush for hours at bridal

Party home footage, purring over "perfect
Weather – cool breeze, clean sunshine"; and the pure
Fact of her pleasure in those grainy tapes
Where maids of honor grinned like prototypes
Of ye olde faithful wife and cummerbund-
Clad groomsmen mocked the ragged cover band
And both of us sat laughing in the frame
While some drunk cousin slurred our uniname
Made clear exactly how our end should start:
A focused visit to the hardware store.
I bought the largest magnet I could find
And held it to the shelved rows of her prized
Home video collection. Love is blind,
Like rage; the facts were facts and had been faced.
To fix her after she had let me go,
I turned the world we'd shared to wind and snow,
Making our story one more shot romance
The power of attraction had erased.

After Watching René Clair's *And Then There Were None*

Okay, to recap: one cat goes kaput
      From sipping poison,
   One biddy overdozes,
      One good old boy's in
  Trouble the moment he sets foot
     Outdoors where he exposes
His back to this flick's Mack the knife (whose ploys in

Each case succeed), one servant who has been
      Grievously taxed –
   Of whom so much of late
     Is asked – is axed
  To death while chopping firewood in
     The yard, and as this spate
Of deaths plays out in spades, tensions are maxed,

And people start confessing: Doc owns up
      To operating
   Drunk, and the judge admits
     To orchestrating
  A false conviction, then the cup
     Passes to one who sits
Wordless before the sentence they're awaiting

Since each has understood the underlying
      Motive for all
   These murders: vigilante
     Justice. All fall
  Short of the glory and, in dying,
     Raise the next hand's ante
For those who'll face the final player's call.

Who doubts our guilt? Who doubts that such divine
          Judgments await?
       Granted, not all of us
         Kill; some just hate,
    Some hiss dissensions, some decline
       To choose the virtuous,
And some display too little good too late,

Yet all the same, should that gray butler play
          A phonograph
       Declaiming our transgressions
         From the least gaffe
    To the most morbidly outré
       Or violent of obsessions,
Who'd doubt that justice corners the last laugh?

Of course, we haven't been enisled without
         A public hearing,
       Nor heard a voice decrying
         All chance of clearing
    Our names, heard gunshots and a shout –
       But there is no denying
That we are, one by one, all disappearing.

Near the Threshold

My shoes are sad. They clump there on the rack,
As dull as monks. Their mouths shape perfect O's.
Singing their one low note, they moan the lack
Of those companions they must now suppose
Will never join the choir: the sneaker hung
From power lines, which everybody knows
Signals a dealer's spot; wet sandals flung
Out of the station wagon, left to freeze;
The mangled work boot. Each shoe lends its tongue
To memory: they drone their elegies
In open grief, their aglets gleam like tears,
Their laces trace morose trajectories –
It's all too human, and it disappears
When, armchaired with dessert, I hear the news
Of workers finding, as the bomb-smoke clears,
Smoldering ankles rising from some shoes
That still have feet in them. Is it unwise
To see in all things grief if grief accrues
So readily? My rows of shoes will rise
In tiers and sing their bone-tired theme,
Each open-mouthed in something like surprise,
Till silence knots their throats as in a dream
Where while you flee fleet creatures at your back,
Your larynx creaks, hinge-like, and you can't scream.

Wake

Here are the random couples bumping uglies,
    And here, prayer circles squeezing hands;
Here are the children curled up in their snugglies,
    And here, tuxedoed bands

Are sweating through their set-to-end-all-sets
    Now that the news of the tsunami
Has been confirmed. God's sent us his regrets
    As global origami –

Sorry, my ducks, this hasn't worked, I fold –
    And now we grow enraged or grave
As we see fit, quaking before the cold
    Wall of God's final wave.

I dreamt all this, bedridden, wrung with heat.
    Since I awoke, I can't erase
The sight of God pulling that huge blue sheet
    Over the world's face.

Degradation

At other times, you manage to forget
The small atrocities, the ambient spite
That still can overwhelm you – how the air
Softened and closed in, like a clump of wet
Cotton across your face, after a fight;
Her canted eyebrow when she would alight
On just the barb to lay your foul soul bare –

And you remember spooning on the futon,
Smooching like teenage newbies half the night
And following some romcom spark for spark,
The dialogue unmoving with the mute on
But needless, really, given your appetite . . .
You led each other, for your own delight,
Into the promise of the semi-dark

As on the screen, the female lead upbraided
Her one-time hubby for some oversight
In cadences like a revival preacher's;
The movie's master tape had so degraded,
However, that her face glowed blinding white,
Lost in the bright bleed of projected light
That had obliterated all her features.

Outtakes (Three Takes)

1. Bad Films

I scorn those flicks where outtakes overtake
The script.
Their actors haven't kept faith with the craft;
Instead, they've laughed,
Burped, tripped,
And biffed their lines as if their famous lives could make

It up to us. They bankroll bankrupt scenes
(Deleted)
And gag reels more engaging than the real
Movies; I feel
Gypped, cheated,
Until I see how our world underwrites the screen's:

Half ceaseless dreams, half momentary drives –
Part grime,
Part grace – we never get the chance to run
Our botched scenes one
More time,
Given how much and long
                 the first take takes our lives.

2. Lost Films

One history of film's the history
Of fire

        [the smoky hole : the perfect
        burnt bull's-eye   in the center

        of the paper : still the best
        testaments   to flame]

    – how many blazes have destroyed
How many feet of priceless celluloid?

       [lyrical nitrate, singing
       its song of immolation]

The nitrate film in use once, chemically
Unstable, could decay or self-ignite;
Huge movie storage vaults were brought to light

       ["my Alexandria . . . my backlit glory . . .
       my haze / and glow, my torch . . ."]

As they, and all their stockpiled masters, went
Up in the smoke of art's most lasting peace.
Not every burned film was a masterpiece,

       ["I could eat alphabet soup
       and shit better lyrics"]

But each of them *is* gone, a permanent
Addition to the roster of the lost.
What's worse, to save on storage space and cost,
Studios sometimes trashed their own film trove,

       ["But if – if, I say – I give in and drop
       this role for another, healthier one, where
       will all the headaches and outtakes go?"]

Especially the silent films they thought
Chic talkies had reduced to diddly-squat
No one would want or watch,

       [glorious aporia, an apologia:
       "English in its billiard-table sense":

language lost in the pockets]

and as they strove
To make the future crisper, louder, clearer,
More lucrative, they lost the silent era
Almost in its entirety,

[the whole   idea was
   the   hole where an idea was]

perhaps
Encouraging by cinememes' mimesis
A glut of glib film theorists in their thesis
That what's important gathers in the gaps
And true chefs-d'oeuvre show where meaning breaks –
Missed takes aren't necessarily mistakes,

[mystics praise detachment]

We're better off with the script scrapped – although
There are those movie-goers who might doubt
That moving films are made by what's left out;
Those viewers still descry a distant glow,
Follow the smell of black smoke, and desire

["cut : perfect!"]

The silent world that set itself on fire.

3. Good Films

I could dissect each frame . . .
But let's talk outtakes. The clip I have in mind
Stalls in the locker room: the cops take aim,

Fire off their lines, and every time, that spritz
Of deodorant across one's chest (aligned
        Just so to douse both pits

        In one long arc) reduces
Them both to fits of giggles. It takes six takes,
Complete with off-screen heckles and snubbed excuses,
To get things right, and now when I review
The real scene, perfectly performed, it makes
        Me chuckle – though they do

        Nothing comedic in
The final cut – because I also see
That string of outtakes as the lines begin;
And those rejected run-throughs, ghostly, rest
Behind the polished product in the free
        Play of a palimpsest.

        I pray God sees us all
That way one day – performances flawless after
Some expert excisions of the unscripted fall
Down stairs or of flubbed lines at misheard cues –
And that he'll give us his forgiving laughter
        And stellar life reviews,

        Glimpsing at once our two
Selves: one who ad-libbed and could never edit
The rough cut; one without a syllable askew.
I pray my life – which can't but intermit –
Will be perfected when I, to my credit,
        Am taken out of it.

At Home

Phlebotinum

Tonight I watch four men get shot
On primetime television: two for narking
On partners, one for love, and one for parking
    In the wrong parking lot

At the wrong time. There follow fifty
Minutes of swift forensic kung fu moves
That culminate in evidence which proves
    These geeks are pretty nifty,

Given that how they nab one crook
Is by enhancing images they find
Reflected in his victim's eyes, a blind
    Luck clue in a last look

Caught by a nearby traffic cam
(No chance); they snag another when they trace
His hairspray through their mystic database
    Of stylists on the lam

(*This* viewer ends up feeling fleeced);
And as for the remaining perps, close shaves
Grow closer till they wind up in their graves –
    Who most risked, counted least

On crime scene gurus also packing
Serious heat and staminaceous bods
That put them little lower than the gods
    (Plus, they get network backing).

My parents lap it up, half-viewing,
Half-reading magazines that track the stars'
Marriages, mansions, children, pooches, cars,
    And causes of undoing,

Reveling in some hard-earned rest
At home behind their thick dead-bolted door.
I've noticed, as they're aging, how much more
    They fear being dispossessed,

And I'd prefer to blame these shows
Where punks are always knocking off a stranger
For pocket change or fun – they posit danger
    As one fixed mark that grows

Only more common with the years –
But Dad says, "Cops or sitcoms, take your pick.
The comedies are worse, they're downright sick,"
    So he prefers his fears.

I found online (also unsafe)
One word encompassing the farthestfetched
Technologies that, in a pinch, are stretched
    To bring a kidnapped waif

Home and her kidnappers to trial,
Saving both victim and the vacant plot –
The serums, powders, pastes, or newly bought
    Dell Inst-o-matic Dial-

Up-DNA, which matches sperm
Samples to cell phone records – and these dumb
Contrivances are called "phlebotinum."
    Now, if I can't confirm

The scientific fact of it,
I know the feeling well: who doesn't crave
A universal solvent fit to save
    Us, make the pieces fit

In every case that we might piece-
meal pass to glory or a second season,
That we might shuck the shackles of our reason
     And feel a new release?

I see my snide analysis
Of crime T.V. as more phlebotinum,
The feeble means by which I try to come
     To terms with all of this,

And now I can't remember where
I heard the story – *Law & Order*? Prime-
time news? – but someone hears the doorbell chime
     And pushes back his chair,

Walks to the peephole and, without
A care, peeks through; thugs shoot him in the eye.
I am afraid of that – that he could die
     Simply by looking out.

Perforated for Ease of Separation

Remember Valentine's in second grade?
The paper bag mailboxes, crinkly hush,
And drugstore cards; the children all afraid
They wouldn't get a single Valentine;
Then, bless their candy hearts, the sugar rush! –
Kids snorting Pixie Stix, the conga line
Parading through the spilled Hawaiian punch,
Time dribbling on until the bell for lunch. . . .

No sane kid wanted to receive the most –
That honor went to someone no one liked
Enough to tease – but almost all could boast
Of five or six good friends and one or two
Secret admirers; and when the children biked
Back home that afternoon, they felt they knew
Their kind acts' exact worth: one juggling clown,
Two jigging ragdolls, and a Charlie Brown.

Maybe you can't quite place the sidelined kid
Who drags a sleeve across his snotty nose
And hides behind the sugar-cube pyramid
While other children blast around the room,
But you do know him: Prince of Grubby Toes
And Funky Lunchbox Smells, the one for whom
A lesson has finally clicked. His shoulders sag.
Love is what fills an empty paper bag.

Zero Percent of Zero

*This idea of doing nothing proves to be absolutely terrifying to mo
people I speak with. But at least the person who is capable of doing
nothing might be capable of refraining from doing the wrong thing.
And then perhaps he or she would be better able to do the right
thing.*

    And doing nothing has many other advantages.

– Dallas Willard

*This is my zero from nature, she said. Zero times anything is zero,
she told the class. Zero wins every fight. Zero demolishes the
world.*

– Aimee Bender

I am intrigued by distance, disappearance,
    Interatomic absences
        Substantiating us,
The empty boxes in a crossword puzzle,
    The inside joke and outside chance,
        The mist of English words
For nonsense – flummery and flim-flam, bunkum,
    Horsefeathers, hogwash, humbug, moonshine,
        Twaddle and poppycock,
Gobbledygook, baloney, balderdash,
    Hokum and hooey, rigmarole,
        Tripe, drivel, tommyrot,
Malarkey, mumbo-jumbo, skimble-skamble,
    And when not one of these will do,
        The grand stultiloquence! –
And why my girlfriend says about a third
    Of what she means. It's emptiness
        That makes the vessel useful,
Somebody famous quipped; my head is useful.
    My heart is, too. What could be worse
        Than half a page of brain-
teasers with all the answers scribbled in?
    Only an orgasm on a talk show.

Give me the cryptogram,
No hint of cipher; give me fog, hard rain,
Blizzards, the proper atmosphere;
Give me the words that mean
The least, those verbal skeleton keys, those picklocks –
Oh, *thing*; oh, *do*. They tell me zero,
The number, was invented
By everyone – the Babylonians,
Mesoamericans, Chinese,
Indians – thereby proving
A lot of nothing, or more expertly phrased,
That plenitude can be a form
Of knowing absolutely
Zippo. I vote for the Chinese, myself:
They have the concept of *wu wei*,
Or action without action,
And I'm particularly adept at that –
Ask the g.f., who does Pilates.
"In Zen Calligraphy,
Wu wei has been represented as a circle,"
Says Wikipedia, a site
That, like them all, exists
Nowhere. The *Tao* is right: the Sage has nothing
To lose if he desires nothing –
That sentence works both ways.
What doesn't work is us. I ask her to
Consider staying, and she says,
"Nope. Nada. No way. Zilch.
Zero percent of zero. Nothing doing."
You want to know the origin
Of all that nonsense? Sure,
Some of the terms have etymologies
As clear as ether: *maamajomboo*,
Mandinka word for "mask"
Or "a masked dancer in religious rites";

Or Buncombe, name of county in
    North Carolina (where
They specialize in bunkum); *poppekak*,
    Which means "doll excrement" in Dutch;
        Or *tripe*, Old French for entrails.
Some sound poetic: *moonshine on the water*,
    The full phrase ran, reminding me
        Of Li Bai's last embrace.
For other terms, we only have surmises –
    A turkey's gobble or a surname
        Of Irish origin
(Mullarkey). Then there are the ones that seem
    To come from – yep, you guessed it – nothing.
        You wonder if I've left
Anything out? Flapdoodle, fiddle-faddle, rubbish.
    The wimpy *piffle*. Blatherskite,
        Codswallop, clap-trap, bosh,
The lyrical unfurl of falderal
    And twiddling thumbs of taradiddle,
        Plus good old-fashioned bullshit.
Sometimes I think I could go on forever.
    She takes a final slug of coffee,
        Grabs her keys, leaves the house;
She somehow walks between the falling snowflakes.
    I stand there in the open doorway,
        A useful, empty space.

The Gift

I've come to value self-
Contained, discretely packaged goods in smaller,
   More manageable portions.

Not that these haven't always
Held fascination for me – when I was
   A child, I loved to pop

Those liquid luminescent
Cold pills through their foil backing; and the best
   Rooms in the museum

Had rows of glowing jars
With fetal pigs and deer and crocodiles,
   Much better than the zoo's

Foul-smelling pens or fake
Savannahs; and I dreamt the bottled dreams
   Of Roald Dahl – but now

It smacks more of pragmatics:
Mild tins of breath mints, travel packs of Kleenex,
   Novels with shorter chapters.

I work a cube job, filling
Out spreadsheets with the data someone else
   Collected, and I take

The subway home. I pry
The frozen corn out of my frozen brownie
   And cook my TV dinner,

Each food in its compartment.
I watch my cookie-cutter sitcoms, read,
   Sleep in a Murphy bed.

Once, for the girl I loved,
I bought three small white bottles – body wash,
    Lotion, and scented oil.

She had been travelling.
I wanted two things: one, to give her something
    Luxuriously indulgent,

And two, to give myself
A good excuse to put my hands all over
    Her body. I could picture

Gliding my thumbs along
Her neck and shoulders, down her back and thighs,
    And everywhere the fragrance

Of jasmine and vanilla,
Which I had chosen because I knew she liked it.
    At least I knew that much.

Alone, I sometimes think
The whole of life is learning how to live
    With memory, or better

Put, learning to survive it.
Do you ignore the time you've lost forever,
    Or do you live it over?

I won't go into details,
But all our visions dissolved before I could
    Surprise her with her gift;

After we parted ways,
I kept those bottles jumbled with my socks,
    Hoping they'd still prove useful –

I would forget about them
For months until the bottles one by one
Grew porous, and a blaze

Of jasmine and vanilla
Invisibly trailed out of the opened drawer,
Scenting the room for days.

Bourbon Aubade

Back when we were all disaffected,
   we oscillated between
      wanting people to

betray no emotion – *stoic as*
   oaks, we repeated, liking
      the ring of its back-

to-back glottal clicks – and wanting more
   people to make spectacles
      of themselves, to break

dance on the sidewalks. We were unique,
   a worn word I no longer
      believe usable

in the plural, just as *a more per-*
   fect union suggests something
      beyond perfection.

Remember, Emily? You used to
   wear black fishnets and lots of
      mascara, scaring

our tight-haired high school teachers out of
   their plaids and tweeds. We were odd,
      loving both mathletes

and poetry, though poetry was
   mostly Ginsberg plus the more
      lubricious cummings,

and when I first told you an aubade
   was a morning song, you heard
      a *u* in morning,

which made sense. What didn't? We made out
   underneath unpicturesque
      trees we didn't know

the names of, you wrote those ironic,
   sentimental ballads on
      a ukulele

you couldn't really play, and we were
   destined to be, despite our
      modesty and means,

the voices of our generation.
   You once told me the foremost
      adaptive strategy

of the human species was pattern-
   making – not perceiving them,
      but creating them

even where there were none – and we did.
   As an inside joke without
      a punch line or pinch

of kindness, we named our suburb's shrubs
   "bourbon trees" and claimed to love
      their fruit because all

this happened before we knew too much
   about plain disappointment
      or dendrology.

I've since learned some aspen stands share one
   underground system of roots:
      they're all the same plant,

they're even called clones. Too perfect. We
   called ourselves *soul mates* back then.
      Make mine a double.

Remember, Em, you are at the heart
   of *remember*. All of this
      happened, and later,

despite our silence, we did become
   voices of our genera-
      tion, like everyone.

Watering the Garden (Till It Bursts into Flame)

Planting impatiens, Charlotte portions out
Her plot's next spots to plants that complement
Impatiens (also known as touch-me-nots).

Me? Neighbor rung to hear her wring harangues
Equally from her best friend's wedded bliss
And weeds that blaze in lazy pyrotechnics

Across the lawn. I listen while I loosen
The hose's brazen nozzle; Charlotte knows
I'll tend to what she's planted, Mr. Handy

Man misting fistfuls of the fitful flowers
She forages and forgets until they wither.
I diamond-dust the lot of them with water

And contemplate the weight of waiting, wanting,
This winter-into-spring song sprung to mind
While minding morning glories, mums, and blooms

Rumored the kissing cousins of jewelweed
Because I hope she finds her passion's match in
(My fair *chère*, share my fire: let every chore

Be tinder tendered to the flames for ages:
Charm me, sweet charlatan: please: char me, Char)
This sexiest of secret potions, patience.

Perfecting Absence

1. Game Theory

… The indispensable, improper fiction
Of your unforgettable perfection.
        – Daryl Hine

After you've met
The wrong girl yet again,
You trudge home tipsily disconsolate
And pray the radio's Top Ten
Provideth you with the keys to retrofit
        Hope to regret,

But plaints by Percy
Sledge taint the airwaves, thick
With strains of thwarted love. How constantly
You've longed to find a (your word) "chick,"
Never imagining your curse might be
        A fine-tuned mercy:

You gravitate
Toward (and I quote) "the ample
Bosoms and bottoms of the world," yet sorrow
To think today's unmatched example
Of Definitely-An-Eight might check tomorrow
        Night's perfect mate –

And that exact
Self-centeredness, that eye for
The (your phrase) "better deal," just proves your fated
Partner – the woman you would die for,
Your unmet soul mate – would be ogled, rated,
        And almanacked

As "one of those
False tarts I dated back
In my expansive, wasted days of shame
    Before I got my life on track"
(Your sentence), one more tipped tile in your game
        Of dominoes.

Not to have crossed
Paths with your Perfect Ten
Before your soul's perfecting has begun
    Breathes mercy time and time again:
The love you haven't found yet is the one
        You haven't lost.

2. Dominus Vobiscum

How shall infection
Presume on thy perfection?
– George Herbert

You'd long suspected
Your love-life's cosmic sweep
Would dominate the headlines, and the day
    Would break when you, at last, could sleep
With willing cultic priestesses who'd allay
        The unperfected

Cosmos's plight
With tantric ministrations
And, tantamount to crowning you the new
    Sun god, would each devise oblations
To raise your caterwauls and cater to
        Your appetite;

And how correct
You were, although you fudged
The form (goodbye, bacchantes! adios,
Associated Press!), misjudged
The function (some big bang!), and simply chose
What you'd expect.

Now you've accumulated, miss by miss,
This litany of girls you'll never kiss,
And started to suspect your own desire
Hints something broader, longer, deeper, higher
Awaits you, one good word in all the garbled
Love songs you've Googled, wondering what was warbled;

And once you're willing (hardly yet aware
Of what has changed), you find yourself in prayer,
That substance that solidifies your days
And makes the very air around you blaze
With meaning – something difficult to parse,
Given how hard its sayings, and how sparse.

There follow weeks of silence. You feel blameless
Before the absent voice, the quell, the flameless
Shrubbery just more shrubbery, forlorn
As winter strips it down to branch and thorn,
The wind unwindpiped, breathing not a word
Of why the Good Lord (q.v.) has demurred.

What do arrive, embodied, are regrets –
Crushed beer cans and extinguished cigarettes,
Stomped party hats, the tatty paperbacks
Stocking the floor in scoliotic stacks,
And even sex reduced to its detritus:
Brief tachycardia, then faint tinnitus.

Here's the conclusion that must be pursued:
If you could barely handle solitude
And wrecked a simple thing like charity,
How could you start expecting ecstasy?
Should God himself grow eager and reveal
His face too soon, you'd want the better deal;

And he, unwilling to permit such loss,
Waits for that moment you're most apt to cross
The chasm spanning pride and caritas,
And only in that kairos moment will
You hear his voice – as promised, small and still –
Filling in you what space there is to fill.

Thus God, in dodging
        Your cataphatic cat-
calls all those years – that God you kept in mind
    Who seemed a catathymic prat –
Did so in the belief he'd one day find
        A proper lodging,

        A perfect shrine
        That needed to be raised
Stone by painstaking stone, however slow –
    However intricately phased –
The raising. Only that way would you know
        The bottom line:

        You're yours to damn;
        To find your sole reprieve
Takes someone else. That someone is inviting –
    At least, so (my words) I believe,
Now when the man I hope to be is writing
        The man I am.

3. Prayer for Reception

I believe in my conscience I intercept many a
thought which heaven intended for another man.
– Laurence Sterne

Father, I'm tired of voices thronging me:
    The love songs throttling the air,
The pop-up spokesmen for eHarmony,
The latest failed romantic comedy
        Arguing happiness
Arises from varieties of undress –
        Truth never looked so bare.

I've tried to fill myself with sounder stuff –
    The Bible, Herbert, and the Bard
To name a few – but how are they enough
To countermine lust's corporate rebuff?
        Could the best thoughts best said,
This harmony of voices in my head,
        Make showing love less hard?

Hence, my retreat. I've tried to concentrate
    On life within a narrowed range,
Thought talking to myself would compensate
For all the silence and the constant state
        Of longing, but I squeeze
So little solace from soliloquies,
        Soulless without exchange.

Father, a not uncommon metaphor –
    The human brain as radio,
The mind as radio waves – seems to me more
Audacious than I've given it credit for.

Which station do I choose?
The one that prompts with ample alleleus
      Never to let you go,

Or that modish other, mocking my denial
      In terms immoderately outspoken?
I can't hear all at once. And some parts fail:
Antennae snap, a diode blows, the dial
      Falls off, and this believer
Needs words that he can hear when the receiver
      Is broken beyond broken,

For I am close now, my equipment's cracked,
      Ship's going down, the S.O.S.
Gushes dit-dashes – circuits wrecked, wits racked –
And only a miracle could counteract
      The physics of this sinking
Feeling, the weighting water, and my thinking
      This radioed distress,

Father, remains unheard; for I am still
      A boy, one prone to these dramatic
Waves of despair, chin on the windowsill,
Twirling the dial, hoping the air will fill
      Midnight with melody,
A changeless love song hurrying to me,
      Ecstatic in the static.

During the Hymn of Commitment

Probably all the choirgirls should be ugly,
But this one isn't, and it makes it hard
To concentrate. She's not my type – too thin
Beneath her choir robe, freckled, hair too short –
But then again, she sings. This morning's anthem
Was *Dies Irae*, which I love and hate.
The Latin thuds along like pickaxe blows,
Unearthing everything I'd like to hold
More closely than – or maybe just against –
The nervous God of if-thine-eye-offend-thee,
Of narrow gates and sheep and goats, God pure
And definite. The singers' voices blend
Terror and triumph at the coming judgment,
And I could take or leave it; what I love
Is the huge minor chord that kicks it off,
As beautiful as thunder if only thunder
Could enter you and rumble through your blood.

The sermon text this morning came from Luke:
"He is not the God of the dead, but of the living."
It should inspire me, but it makes me think
Of Tennyson's most terrifying line:
'Farewell! We lose ourselves in light.' Imagine
A prism working backward, taking all
Those gorgeous, separate beams – the sweet, bold red
Of some girl's dream bike, greens in the exact
Shades of a high school diary she lost,
The liquor-bottle blue of her favorite dress –
And crushing them together, muddling them
Until they have become the blank white light
In textbook photographs, and the result is
Tennyson's dreaded general soul. I'm good
At fear, but that's just masterful: to be
Afraid of darkness is a simple thing,
But to discover fearfulness in light?

A line like that one proves that if you choose
To look more carefully at what you love,
You'll always find a little more to lose.
I've wondered if the obverse would obtain –
Something about observing what you hate
Until you find how much there is to gain.

I'd say that God must look at us both ways
Except I don't believe that; only love
Could possibly explain such depths of anger,
The way that I am angry when I think
Of having to abandon certain things.
There's nothing that I wouldn't want to keep.
Walking one afternoon, I saw three crows
Perched on a barbecue grill like three sleek gargoyles,
Sifting through ash to feed on what was left
Of the charred chunks of meat that someone let
Drop through the grate. Devotion, of a kind.

Last night while reading, I discovered Greek
Has one more word for "love" than I had thought:
Storgē: instinctive love. It made me wonder
What other words we're missing, whether some
Endangered language has a word that means,
"To love someone for who she's going to be,"
Or one that means, "to love a stranger more
Than someone you have known your entire life,"
Or one that means, "to love until you're damned."
The one I really want would name this instant,
When everyone is singing – loudly, badly –
One of my favorite hymns, "Just As I Am,"
And I am thinking exactly what I thought
During the anthem: she is beautiful,
And I believe I somehow hear above
The myriad, blending voices just her voice.

The Pocket Watch

My grandpa was the king of disappearing
Small household goods – a cough drop or a penny,
A handkerchief, a knitting needle, any
Number of knickknacks, Uncle Kevin's hearing
Aid – but he'd always bring them back in time
To rustle up his daily rum and Coke.
I loved it when he'd whisper, *Let's go for broke;*
He'd zilch that penny and give me back a dime.

He had two silver crowns and skinny legs.
No wand, no cape. He was an amateur
With one perfected trick, but I was sure
One day he would unscramble broken eggs
Or saw my Gram, his "better half," in half
And put her back together, which would prove
His mastery of more than one slick move.
The whole room laughed whenever he would laugh.

He went to pieces when my grandma died.
The weekend of her funeral, I found him
Beating his pocket watch against the ground.
Look at this thing, he hissed. *Look. Look inside.*
He skittered it to me, and underneath
The mangled face and one remaining hand
I saw the gears. *You get it? Understand?*
Never trust anything with that many teeth.

The One Idea

The theopathic Trappist feels
His one idea – God – conceals
The hope that every syndrome heals,
        But when a schism
Invites the violence proving zeal's
        Fanaticism,

He might feel tempted to discard
His one idea and regard
All single-mindedness as marred
        By taking sides:
Any thought thought so long and hard
        Quickly divides.

If pain's the thought we take apart –
The broken hip or broken heart –
We call it anguish, then, or art
        (That difference shrinking
Depending on how shapely, smart,
        Or pained our thinking).

With other ideas, it's the same:
What starts as pleasure, wealth, or fame,
Thought solely, earns another name –
        Indulgence, greed,
Self-centeredness – until each aim
        Becomes raw need,

A thought its thinker can't outwit;
And sweetness cannot salvage it,
Since even sweet fruit boasts a pit –
        A prophet focused
So fiercely on the honey bit
        He skipped the locust

Would drizzle honey on all things
(Honey on stones, on sticks, on stings)
And thereby sacrifice his wings
    For a sweet timbre
That trapped the truth in ramblings
    Like ants in amber.

And what of truth? Does it, too, split
When we, in truth, examine it?
The views, thus far, are disparate;
    We can't agree
If history is adequate
    To memory.

There's only one unmitigated
Concept on which I've meditated,
Hoping it might, unmediated,
    Drop from above;
I'm thinking of the elevated
    Concept of love.

But even that thought circles back
To lust, obsession, an attack
Of madness, an abundant lack,
    And, classically,
A grave cerebro-cardiac
    Pathology,

A tune one whistles in the cold,
A backward alchemy (from gold
To lead), a charm, a line one's sold –
    And what's most odd,
If God is love (and so I'm told),
    Then love is God,

And in the mental whirligig
Of contemplating that enig-
ma, I resist this paradig-
      ma, as I should.
With one idea, better be big.
      Better be good.

Now, if a farmer chose to break
A new well's ground beside a lake,
Fell in the hole he meant to make,
      And – once he fell –
Continued with the same mistake
      Till all was well,

We wouldn't praise him for his sound
Judgment in breaking just that ground
Or call him great; we'd call him drowned.
      Shouldn't a thought
As thorough as that hole be found
      As like as not?

There's only one idea rich
And true enough – like perfect pitch –
That it gets thought without a hitch:
      Nothing, as it's
The one idea into which
      Everything fits.

The Album at the World's End

I think how, at the world's end, all
Our shortfalls – flights and chances missed,
Lost months and causes, mouths unkissed,
       The uncorrected
Proofs of the lives we couldn't call
Our own, our private *Iliads'*
Vast catalogues of never-hads –
       Could be collected

And pasted into scrapbooks full
Of who we weren't but who we might
Have been if we'd had better light
       Or hands more even;
And paging through the possible,
Pacing faint paths we left behind
For those we chose, we might just find
       A kind of heaven,

An endlessness of selves that live
Forever in the unbegun
(Which can't be done if never done),
       Who rarely strike us
As shabby or uncooperative,
Insanely dull or prone to snore:
We love our own eidolons more
       The less they're like us.

Let me repeat this, love, once more:
I know our heartache, part by part,
Gave far more ache than we had heart;
       Yet I'd still trade
That album at the world's end for
(However plain, however brief,
However full of pain and grief)
       The one we made.

Bachelor Pad

He took it with him everywhere he went,
    The small green notebook with the lock.
He wanted to compile a permanent
        Log of the pillow talk,
Endearments, jokes, evasions, gentle lies
    And not so gentle ones, mute clock-
Watching, brisk whispers, shrugs, outbursts and sighs
        From every argument
Couples engaged in right before his eyes.

He had decided on nothing with designs,
    A notebook unbedrecked or -jeweled;
As for the paper, some folks wanted lines,
        But he preferred unruled.
He'd riffle through a paperback for cover,
    Hoping he had the barroom fooled
(Just reading . . .) while his ballpoint pen would hover
        To catch whatever wines
Or whiskeys might elicit from a lover.

Soon couples stumbled out – pansophic, sloshed –
    And nights packed up. He'd head for home,
And there, amidst the mismatched forks, unwashed
        Boxers, and Styrofoam
Go-boxes seeping in the fridge, he'd think
    Of an enormous marbled comb
(Brown), empty glass (blue), soap (tan), matchstick (pink,
        Yellow), and brush (brown) squashed
Inside – and thereby dwarfing – a rinky-dink

Apartment too much like the one he had;
    Magritte had called it *Personal
Values*, but could have called it *Bachelor Pad*
        For all that it was full
Of looming objects – eerie, bulksome, sly.

He worried that he lived his whole
Life in his notebook, and he wondered why
    That didn't seem so bad.
(Sometimes the room looked more like open sky.)

Often he'd scan his notes as though they formed
    A star chart, score, or recipe,
An atlas of lands battered and bestormed,
    Or an anatomy
Textbook (we're all one body, he has read);
    And whether lost in bodily
Desire, on lush paths, in rhapsodies of dread
    Or soups he'd barely warmed,
He hummed his praise for starlight overhead.

His notebook boggled: proverbs, quips, wish lists,
    Points, counterpoints, élan, chagrin –
Everything from the televangelist's
    "*Single* begins with *sin!*"
(*But so does sing*, he couldn't help include)
    To Tillich's key distinction in
A timely sermon: for days we brink and brood,
    Our *loneliness* exists;
For hours of glory, we have our *solitude*.

O, fond farrago, book of quodlibets,
    You awful gallimaufry plumb
Full of hysteria's careless ariettes,
    You solemn omnium
Gatherum of God's wisdom, sottisier
    Of teasing bits' bêtises, you come
Down to this question – will love's gets outweigh
    Love's *quod erat* regrets? –
And how to answer that, he couldn't say;

But from that blitz and clutter, his helter-skelter
    Homage, he prized a single image:
A couple. Thick rain. A tiki bar for shelter.
    The girlfriend stared at him,
Her boyfriend – blabbering as he chased a benny
    With vodka, bar-wise to the brim –
As though he were a wishing well, and when he
    Paused, somewhere in the welter
Of copper wishes, she sought her lonely penny.

He couldn't judge the lovers with their cosmos
    And appletinis, none of them –
Men numb with *Maxims*, women lost in *Cosmos*
    Dog-eared with stratagem –
He loved the whole damn lot, since he could see
    The grounds from which their longings stem:
Forces as grave, expansive, dark and free
    As any where a cosmos
Begins in utter singularity.

Notes

One Table Over   "Tetelestai" is a Greek word meaning, "It is finished." In commercial contexts, it signified that a bill or debt had been paid.

Small Change   I owe thanks to Kelsey Vogel for this poem.

Lana Turner's Bosom: An Assay   I read the anecdote about Lana Turner in Jeanine Basinger's marvelous book *The Star Machine*.

For details about the Leo Frank case, I am indebted to the author mentioned, Steve Oney, and his excellent book, *And the Dead Shall Rise: The Murder of Mary Phagan and the Lynching of Leo Frank*. Any factual errors in my poetic deployment of the details of the case belong to me, of course, and not to Mr. Oney.

In addition to spawning *Death in the Deep South*, the Ward Greene novel upon which *They Won't Forget* was based, the Phagan-Frank tragedy also inspired two Oscar Micheaux films, *The Gunsaulus Mystery* (lost) and *Murder in Harlem* (at the time of this writing, available on the Internet Archive at www.archive. org); a TV miniseries, *The Murder of Mary Phagan*; a David Mamet novel, *The Old Religion*; a PBS film, *The People v. Leo Frank*; and a musical, *Parade*. I'm sure there are other fictional treatments.

Outtakes (Three Takes)   The quoted texts in the second section are lines from "Chanteuse" by Mark Doty, a quip by Johnny Mercer about a popular musical, lines from "Love's Passing" by Rachel Wetzsteon, and a remark by James Merrill. The final quoted fragment is notional.

Lyrical Nitrate is the name of a collage film by Peter Delpeut; it consists of various clips from silent films that used the now-deteriorating nitrate film stock.

In the third section, the outtake being described comes from the film *Hot Fuzz*.

During the Hymn of Commitment   The speaker of this poem references Luke 20:38, which follows a discussion of whether or not people will be married after the resurrection. (They will not.) The Tennyson poem referenced is *In Memoriam,* XLVII.

Bachelor Pad Paul Tillich's "timely sermon" is called "Loneliness and Solitude" and can be found in *The Eternal Now*.

A Note About the Author

Stephen Kampa was born in Missoula, Montana, in 1981 and grew up in Daytona Beach, Florida. He received a BA in English Literature from Carleton College and an MFA in Poetry from the Johns Hopkins University. His first book, *Cracks in the Invisible*, won the 2010 Hollis Summers Poetry Prize and the 2011 Gold Medal in Poetry from the Florida Book Awards. His poems have also been awarded the Theodore Roethke Prize, first place in the *River Styx* International Poetry Contest, and two Pushcart nominations. He currently divides his time between teaching poetry at Flagler College in St. Augustine, Florida and working as a musician, most recently with Florida swamp blues master Robert "Top" Thomas and as a session player for WildRoots Records.

OTHER BOOKS FROM WAYWISER

*Co-published with Picador